India

Tom Streissguth

✺ Carolrhoda Books, Inc. / Minneapolis

Photo Acknowledgments

Photos, maps and artworks are used courtesy of John Erste, pp. 1, 2–3, 8–9, 11, 23, 39, 42–43; Laura Westlund, pp. 4–5, 27; © Air India Library, pp. 6, 36 (bottom); © Trip/H. Rogers, pp. 7, 9, 17 (top), 18 (bottom), 20, 23, 29; © Jean S. Buldain, pp. 8–9, 12 (bottom), 25 (bottom); © Courtesy of Embassy of Pakistan, p. 10; © Trip/Dinodia, pp. 11, 14, 15, 19, 24, 43 (bottom); © Trip/T. Bognar, p. 12 (top); © John Elk, pp. 12 (middle), 21; © American Lutheran Church, pp. 16, 34; © Brian Vikander, pp. 17 (bottom), 44; © Trip/Resource Foto, pp. 18 (top), 30; © Gerald Cubitt, p. 22; © Trip/B. Turner, p. 25 (top); © Agence France Presse/Corbis–Bettmann, p. 26; © Courtesy of Minneapolis Public Library and Information Center, p. 27; © Don Eastman, p. 28; © Michele Burgess, pp. 31, 32 (both); © Trip/B. Vikander, p. 33; © Tony Tigwell, p. 35; © TG Malhotra/Visuals Unlimited, p. 36 (top); © Trip/P. Rauter, p. 37; © Dinodia Picture Agency/Ravi Shekhar, pp. 38, 41; © Trip/W. Jacobs, p. 39; © Beverly Arenz, p. 40; © Trip/C. Wormald, p. 42; © Trip/B. Gibbs, p. 43 (top); © Dinodia Picture Agency, p. 45. Cover photo of people bathing in Ganges, © Michele Burgess.

Carolrhoda Books, Inc.
c/o The Lerner Publishing Group
241 First Avenue North
Minneapolis, Minnesota 55401 U.S.A.

Website address: www.lernerbooks.com

Words in **bold type** are explained in a glossary that begins on p. 44.

Library of Congress Cataloging-in-Publication Data

Streissguth, Thomas, 1958–
    India / by Tom Streissguth
        p.   cm. — (Globe-trotters club)
    Includes index.
    Summary: An overview of India emphasizing its cultural aspects.
    ISBN 1-57505-111-7 (lib.bdg.: alk. paper)
    1. India—Juvenile literature. [1. India.] I. Title II. Series:
Globe-trotters club (series)
DS407.S86 1999
954—DC21
                                             97-2699

Manufactured in the United States of America
1 2 3 4 5 6 – JR – 04 03 02 01 00 99

Contents

Swagatam Bharat-Varsh!   4

Mountains Crash! Bang!   6

Holy Rivers!   8

First Indians   10

A Land of Many Cultures   12

Your Language or Mine?   14

It's Crowded Here!   16

Religions of Choice   18

Caste of Players   20

A House in the Country   22

A Population Problem   24

Old and New Indias   26

Family Matters   28

Dig In!   30

Getting Dressed   32

Going to School   34

Nights with Lights   36

Crazy about Cricket   38

Lights! Camera! Action!   40

Indian Music   42

Glossary   44

Pronunciation Guide   46

Further Reading   47

Index   48

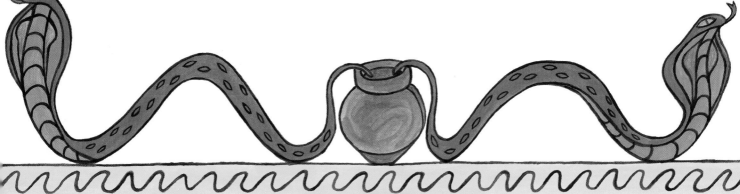

Swagatam **Bharat-Varsh!***

* That's "Welcome to India" in Hindi, one of the official languages of India.

CHINA

Indus River

PAKISTAN

• Srinagar

H
I
M
A
L
A
Y
A
S

NEPAL

Mt.
Kanchenjunga

BHUTAN

Harappa ■

PUNJAB

New Delhi
★

Ganges River

ASSAM

Mohenjo-
Daro ■

Jodhpur •

INDO-GANGETIC

DESERT
OF THAR

Jaipur •

Varanasi •

PLAIN

MYANMAR
(BURMA)

I N D I A

Calcutta

BANGLADESH

Mumbai
(Bombay) •

D E C C A N

PLATEAU

W
E
S
T
E
R
N

G
H
A
T
S

E
A
S
T
E
R
N

G
H
A
T
S

ARABIAN
SEA

Hyderabad •

*BAY OF
BENGAL*

Bangalore •

N

Madras

TAMIL
NADU

SRI LANKA

INDIAN OCEAN

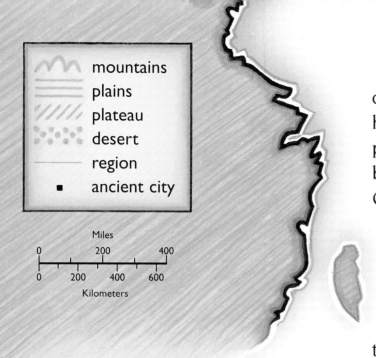

mountains
plains
plateau
desert
region
■ ancient city

Miles

0   200   400

0   200   400   600

Kilometers

of Bangladesh that looks a bit like a hiker trekking into Myanmar? That's part of India, too. India's southern border is much less complicated. Ocean waters lap against most of it. The Bay of Bengal, part of the Indian Ocean, lies to the east, and the Arabian Sea borders India on the west. Off the southeastern tip of India sits Sri Lanka, a large teardrop-shaped island.

If you were to go to every country in the world, you would see only six bigger than India. In fact India and its smaller neighbors almost make up a continent, or big patch of land, of their own. That's why India and the countries around it are sometimes called the Indian **subcontinent.**

On a map of the world, India looks kind of like a diamond. Pakistan, Nepal, Bhutan, Myanmar (once called Burma), Bangladesh, and China (including Tibet) touch India in the north. But don't forget about the rest of India. See the land east

It's Greek to Me...

The Hindi word for India is Bharat. Where did the word India come from? The ancient Greeks gave this name to the land beyond the Indus River. The Greeks first came through India with Alexander the Great about 2,300 years ago.

5

Mountains **Crash! Bang!**

Picture this! Millions of years ago, India and Australia were part of one huge island in the Indian Ocean. The island eventually broke apart. India floated north, where it collided with Asia, and Australia sailed away to the southeast.

When India crashed into Asia, the Himalayas buckled up between them. The Himalayas are the highest mountains in the world. The highest point in the Indian Himalayas is a peak named Kanchenjunga. (Mount Everest, also in the Himalayas, is located on the border between Nepal and Tibet.)

Just south of the Himalayas is the lush, flat Indo-Gangetic **Plain.** The plain is named after the two rivers that surround it—the Ganges, which runs through northern India, and the Indus, which flows westward, through Pakistan. Not all of the plain is green, though. The **Desert** of Thar in northwestern India gets only 10 inches of rain each year!

In the middle of India, the Deccan **Plateau** separates the Western Ghat from the Eastern Ghat. The Ghats are mountain chains that run along the coasts.

Fast Facts about India

Name: Bharat (Republic of India)
Area: 1.3 million square miles
Main Landforms: Himalaya Mountains, Indo-Gangetic Plain, Desert of Thar, Deccan Plateau, Eastern Ghats and Western Ghats
Highest Point: Kanchenjunga (28,146 feet)
Lowest point: Sea level
Animals: Asian elephants, Bengal tigers, spotted deer, antelopes, mongooses, wild buffalo, peacocks, hornbills, king cobras, macaques, crocodiles
Capital City: New Delhi
Other Major Cities: Mumbai (Bombay), Calcutta, Varanasi, Hyderabad, Madras, Bangalore, Srinagar
Official Languages: Hindi, English
Money Unit: Rupee

(Opposite page) **The snowy Himalayas stretch for 1,500 miles across northern India.** (Left) **It's a bumpy ride, but camels are one of the best ways to cross the Desert of Thar.**

Holy Rivers!

Boaters on the Ganges River row past the crowded waterfront of Varanasi, a city in northeastern India.

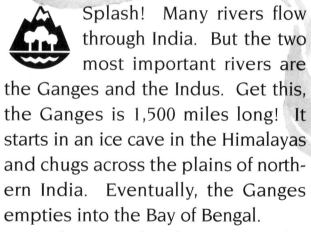

Splash! Many rivers flow through India. But the two most important rivers are the Ganges and the Indus. Get this, the Ganges is 1,500 miles long! It starts in an ice cave in the Himalayas and chugs across the plains of northern India. Eventually, the Ganges empties into the Bay of Bengal.

Hindus, people who practice the religion of Hinduism, believe that the Ganges River is special. Every day thousands of people bathe in its waters. They crowd the river's banks on steps called the **ghats** at the holy city of Varanasi. Sick people touch the water, hoping that it will cure them. Hindus even go to the Ganges to die. They believe people who die in the river will go to paradise.

The Indus River only cuts across a small portion of northern India, but

8

Winds of Change

Winds called **monsoons** determine the weather in India. In the summer and early fall, the monsoons blow from the southwest. The winds bring heavy rain along for the ride. Many farmers depend on the monsoon rains to water their crops. If rains come too late or if it rains too much, entire fields can be wiped out.

Standing on stone steps called ghats, many Hindu and Jain religious believers start their day with a bath in the sacred Ganges.

it played a big part in bringing the first inhabitants to the country. Ancient Indians called the Indus "King River" because it watered their crops. The river's rich valley was also the hub of a civilization that prospered from 2500 B.C. until 1700 B.C.

First
Indians

In 1922 scientists unearthed the ruins at Mohenjo-Daro, an ancient city in the Indus River valley. The ruins still hold secrets of people who lived there long ago.

The most ancient of all Indian people are the Adivasi, a group who lived in India more than 4,500 years ago. They lived in all parts of India until two groups, the Dravidians and the Aryans, invaded and pushed the Adivasi into remote areas of the country, where they still live.

The Dravidians built more than 300 villages and towns in the Ganges and Indus River valleys of northern India and eastern Pakistan. Ruins at the ancient cities of Harappa and Mohenjo-Daro show that people lived in brick homes on carefully planned streets. People in these cities farmed for a living and used written numbers and letters.

A group of people from the northwest called the Aryans swept into the Indus River valley 1,000 years later. The Aryans pushed the Dravidians from their homeland and into southern India. The Aryans spoke and wrote in the ancient language of Sanskrit.

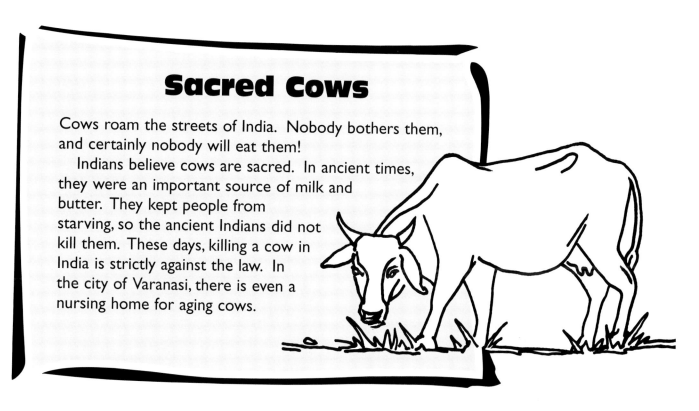

Sacred Cows

Cows roam the streets of India. Nobody bothers them, and certainly nobody will eat them!

Indians believe cows are sacred. In ancient times, they were an important source of milk and butter. They kept people from starving, so the ancient Indians did not kill them. These days, killing a cow in India is strictly against the law. In the city of Varanasi, there is even a nursing home for aging cows.

There are about 50 million Adivasi in India. The Adivasi follow their own customs, which have remained unchanged for hundreds of years.

A Land **of Many Cultures**

Women from the northwestern state of Rajasthan shop for groceries at the market.

Two boys from Madurai in Tamil Nadu smile for the camera.

These two children live in Kashmir. Their family is Muslim, and they practice the religion of Islam.

These days Dravidians and Aryans make up the two major **ethnic groups** in India. Descendants of the early Dravidians still live in the south and form the country's largest group.

India has many smaller ethnic groups, too. The members of each group share a common language or religion. The Tamils, for example, whose ancestors are Dravidian, speak Tamil and tend to live in the southern state of Tamil Nadu. More than 12 million Sikhs make their homes in the northwestern state of Punjab and have their own religion. Can you guess what it's called? Sikhism! Sikhs speak an Indo-Aryan language called Punjabi. Bengalis live in northeastern India in the state of West Bengal and in Bangladesh. They speak Bengali. All in all, about 16 percent of the world's people live in India.

Meeting and Greeting in India

Indians generally don't shake hands. Instead, when meeting someone, they use the *namaste*. They bring their palms together in front of their chest, with their fingers pointing upward. They say "namaste," which means "I bow to thee," and make a pranam (a slight bow), toward the other person. Try it!

Your Language **or Mine?**

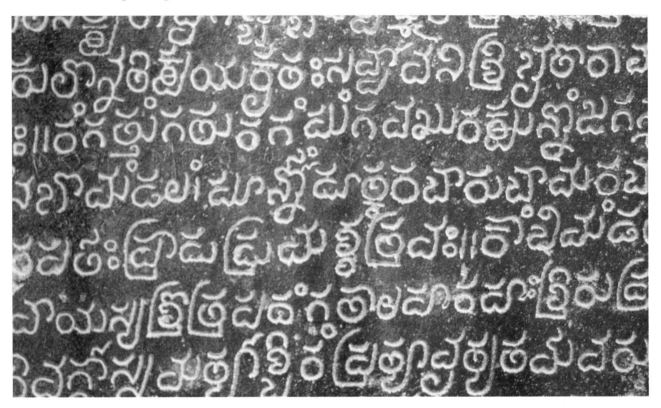

An example of Brahmi script from a sign in Saranth

Have you ever tried to talk to someone who doesn't speak your language? It's not easy. That's why Indians who speak the same language or **dialect** (local language) like to live close to one another. In fact many Indian states are named after the language most spoken by the people who live there.

The two official languages in India are English and Hindi, but there are 16 national languages, and more than 1,600 different dialects. Most of these languages—like Hindi, Bengali, and Gujarati—developed from ancient languages that Aryans brought to India. Languages such as Tamil, Kannada, Telugu, and Malayalam came from the Dravidians.

Most Indians in the north speak Hindi, which is related to ancient Sanskrit. The states of Bihar, Madhya Pradesh, Rajasthan, and Uttar Pradesh are called the "Hindi Belt." Hindi films have helped to spread the language around the country in modern times. But in the south, many people don't want to speak Hindi, even though the government hopes to make it the national language. Many southerners choose to speak Tamil, English, or another local language instead. People fear that if they are forced to learn Hindi, their regional language will die out.

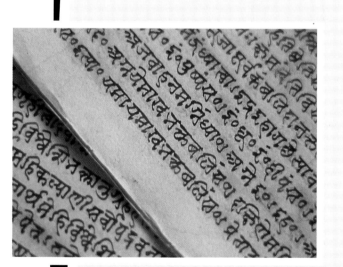

Ancient Language

One of India's languages is Sanskrit. Nobody speaks Sanskrit anymore, but some people can still read it. Famous stories like the sacred books of Hinduism and the favorite Indian folk epic, the *Bhagavad-Gita,* are written in Sanskrit.

Hindi uses the same alphabet as Sanskrit. This alphabet, called *divanagari,* has 33 consonants and 13 vowels. Each letter represents a certain sound. The letters of single words in this alphabet are linked with a line across the top.

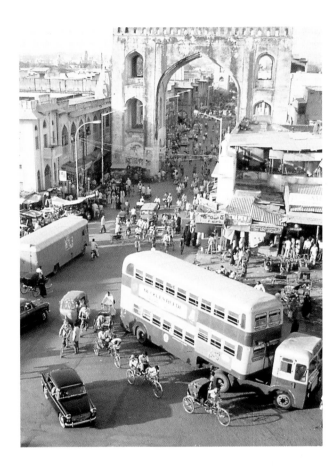

It's Crowded **Here!**

How does your family get around? Most Indians rely on bicycles, motorbikes, taxis, or their feet. Very few families in India have their own car. It's usually faster to walk or ride a bike any-

way. You wouldn't believe the crowds! People, cattle, bicycles, push carts, and wagons crowd the streets. Car drivers lean out their windows and shout for those in front to clear the road.

For long distances, people take a train or a bus. Chickens, dogs, cats, and even goats climb on board for the trip.

Where two roads meet, vendors often set up tea shops and sell drinks to travelers. Sometimes there's even a small shrine at a crossroads, dedicated to Ganesh, the god who keeps travelers safe. (A shrine is a sacred place that may contain religious images.) People leave offerings and pray for protection during their journey.

Trains are sometimes so packed that passengers have to ride on the roof!

It's not unusual to see people piled on top of an overflowing bus in Calcutta.

Ganesh

Ganesh is the Hindu god of wealth and wisdom. He also protects travelers. Shrines to Ganesh show him with the head of an elephant. Here's the legend.

Ganesh's father, Shiva, went away on a long journey. When he came back, he found a man in his house. He immediately chopped off the man's head. Shiva didn't know that the man was his grown-up son.

Shiva's wife, Parvati, got very angry. She forced him to bring their son back to life. He could do it, but he had to use the head of the first animal he saw. The animal was an elephant.

Religions of
Choice

(Right) **A Buddist monk prays at a temple in Sarnath. Less than 1 percent of Indians practice Buddhism.** (Below) **A Hindu woman in Calcutta, India, purifies the Ganges by spreading goddess flowers on its surface.**

Indians practice any one of many different religions—including Islam, Buddhism, Sikhism, Jainism, and Christianity. But eight out of ten Indians follow Hinduism and are called Hindus. (Don't be confused! Hindi is a language. A Hindu is a religious believer.) Many Indians learn about religion from their mothers. When they are still very young, most children hear long stories from the

Ramayana or the *Mahabharata*, the two ancient stories of Hinduism.

Hindus believe in a supreme soul of the universe called the Brahman. All souls eventually return to the Brahman, but first a Hindu must pass through many earthly lives. A man is born, dies, and is reincarnated, or reborn. He might come back as a woman, a cat, a cow, or any other living thing. This cycle of death and rebirth is called *karma*. In each life, a Hindu has certain duties, called *dharma*.

Jainism

A teacher named Mahavira founded Jainism in India in the 500s B.C. Those who follow Jainism believe that every living thing has a soul (called the jiva) that lives on forever in a temporary body. The jiva becomes trapped in the body by everyday activities. To free the jiva, a person must lead a very simple life. Jivas are reborn many times into different bodies before they are finally freed.

Untouchables make up 15 percent of the Indian population. As outcastes of society, the often live together in small communities.

Caste **of Players**

All Hindus and Jains believers belong to a **caste.** A caste is a social group that holds a traditional place in Hindu or Jain culture. There may be a few hundred people in a caste or millions. In all more than 2,000 castes exist.

People are born into their caste, and they can't switch to another. Many rules govern caste behavior. People from different castes can't eat together. They can't attend the same **shrine** or even draw water from the same well. Millions of Hindus don't belong to any caste at all.

Known as untouchables, they are stuck on the lowest rung of the social ladder. To escape the caste system, some untouchables have switched to Buddhism, a religion that doesn't have castes. Even though India outlawed the caste system nearly 50 years ago, most people still follow it. The caste system remains especially strong in rural villages, where the majority of Indians live.

Varnas

India's castes are divided into four groups called varnas. Certain jobs are linked to each caste. Brahmans are priests and teachers. Kshatriyas are soldiers, rulers, and administrators. Vaisyas are merchants and craftspeople. Sudras are farmers and laborers.

This *sadu,* or male Hindu pilgrim (wanderer), comes from the highest caste of Brahmans. Sadus give up everything to devote themselves to their faith.

21

A House in the Country

About 8 out of every 10 Indians make their homes in the countryside. Most live in villages in houses made of clay, brick, or even palm leaves. (When it's hot, the leaves can be lifted off the walls to cool down the house.)

Traditional homes have a porch in front and an open courtyard in the middle. Family members spend much of their time in the courtyard, where they eat, work, read, and talk. On hot nights, the whole family sleeps in the courtyard on *charpoys*, wooden beds made of rope netting. It's like one big slumber party!

Many dads leave the village each morning to work on their farm. Depending on where they live, farmers may grow rice, wheat, tea, cotton, tobacco, coffee, or sugar. Farming is hard work. That's why couples who live in the country have a lot of children. After their schooling is over, children work on the family farm.

Take a peek inside this northern country home. The kids are sitting on a charpoy.

Near Jodhpur, India, a woman and her baby take in some sun in their family courtyard. Homes in this part of the country are built with the red clay that is plentiful here.

Shoes Outside!

A neat row of shoes and sandals sits in front of many Indian homes. Apartment dwellers set their shoes on wooden racks outside the building. Indians view shoes as unclean because they touch dirty streets all day. Everyone takes off footwear before entering a home.

In the house, people walk barefoot. And they are always careful what they do with their feet. In India showing the bottom of your feet to someone is considered very rude.

A *Population* Problem

How crowded is India? Imagine all of your family members living in your house. Add 160 people per family member. Jam packed, isn't it? That's what it's like to live in Calcutta, India, where 79,000 people live in each urban square mile. More than 900 million people live in India. Even though most Indians live in small villages, the country's cities, like Calcutta, Mumbai (modern Bombay), and New Delhi, each have more than 5 million people!

So many people using city resources causes big problems. Indian city dwellers have to deal with power outages and water shortages. Many families keep a full water tank on top of their house in case of an emergency.

Rows of squatter homes fill the slums, or poor neighborhoods, in Mumbai, India.

Homeless people make themselves as comfortable as they can on a Calcutta street.

But some people don't even have a house to call their own. Because there are not enough apartments or homes for everyone, thousands of people sleep in the streets. Squatters—people without homes—live just outside of the cities. They build their shelters out of cardboard or scrap metal.

Shoppers work their way through a crowded market in New Delhi's Old City.

Old and New Indias

In New Delhi, both modern satellite dishes and the Jama Masjid temple, built in the 1600s, crowd the skyline. These days satellite dishes have sprouted from the rooftops of many Indian homes.

India has one of the oldest cultures in the world. Temples built hundreds of years ago dot the countryside. But India also has computers, rockets, nuclear power, freeways, skyscrapers, and the Internet, too.

Many Indians jump back and forth between the ancient and the modern world each day. At home they live by traditional customs. They follow ancient rituals during religious services and festivals. They arrange marriages for their sons and daughters.

At work they communicate with portable telephones and personal computers. Some families also buy electronic gadgets for their homes. City dwellers are able to watch television by satellite. Jet airplanes will take them to other countries.

At times the two sides of India clash. There are conflicts over how

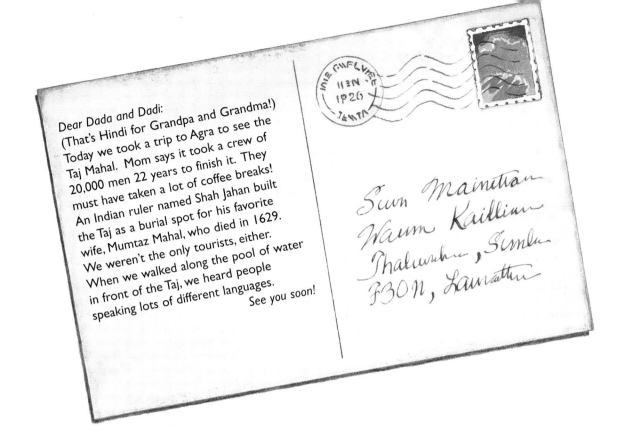

Dear Dada and Dadi:
(That's Hindi for Grandpa and Grandma!)
Today we took a trip to Agra to see the
Taj Mahal. Mom says it took a crew of
20,000 men 22 years to finish it. They
must have taken a lot of coffee breaks!
An Indian ruler named Shah Jahan built
the Taj as a burial spot for his favorite
wife, Mumtaz Mahal, who died in 1629.
We weren't the only tourists, either.
When we walked along the pool of water
in front of the Taj, we heard people
speaking lots of different languages.
See you soon!

to dress, how to work, even how to greet another person. Every day people must decide how to observe customs of the past, while living in a hectic modern world.

The Taj Mahal, on the banks of the Yamuna River, is made entirely of white marble. Four tall prayer towers, called minarets, rise around the Taj's dome-topped main building.

An Indian farm family gathers in front of their home near the northern Indian town of Jaipur.

Family **Matters**

A trip to grandma's house can be very short in some Indian families. Many people don't even have to leave home! Indian kids usually share a home with a few brothers and sisters, their parents, their grandparents, and sometimes even their aunts and uncles. Sounds like fun, huh?

An Indian household gets even bigger when sons grow up and get married. In India marriage is thought to be more of a link between two families than a bond between two people. That's why parents often arrange the marriages of their children. When the couple is first married, they live with the husband's family until they can afford their own apartment or house.

All in the Family

Here are some Hindi words for members of the family. Practice using these terms on your own family. See if they can understand you!

grandfather	*dada*	(dah-DAH)
grandmother	*dadi*	(dah-DEEH)
father	*pita*	(pi-TAAH)
mother	*mata*	(mah-TAAH)
uncle	*chacha*	(CHAH-chah)
aunt	*chachi*	(CHAH-cheeh)
son	*beta*	(bae-TAH)
daughter	*beti*	(BAE-teeh)
brother	*bahai*	(BHAA-ee)
sister	*bahan*	(BE-ha-nh)

In many Indian families, parents still arrange the marriages of their children. They may search for a long time for the right husband or wife for their child.

Looks good enough to eat, doesn't it? A spice called turmeric makes rice dishes yellow, while peppers and curry spice things up.

Dig **In!**

Āpré khā liyā? That's "Have you eaten?" in Hindi. Everybody gathers around a low table and takes a seat on a cushion.

What's on the menu? A spicy sauce called **curry** seasons many Indian foods. To make curry, cooks grind spices like cinnamon and cardamom in a small stone bowl called a mortar. They mix these spices into a paste made from mashed vegetables like pumpkin, squash, or lentils (a cousin of the pea). Tasty curries flavor meat, vegetable, or fish dishes. But be careful! A curry can be spicy hot. If it burns your tongue, eat some fruit or yogurt—water won't help!

Most Indians eat their meals with their fingers, rolling meat, vegetables, and curry into a flatbread called *chapati*. It's considered perfectly okay to lick the fingers, to chew loudly, to clean your teeth, or to burp during the meal.

Whole Wheat Flatbread: Chapati

In northern India, most meals are served with dal, a thick dipping sauce made from lentils, and a flat wheat bread called chapati.

You will need:
1 1/2 cups whole wheat flour
2 tablespoons softened butter or margarine, cut into small pieces
1 teaspoon salt dissolved in 1 cup lukewarm water

1. In a large mixing bowl, rub butter into 2 cups flour with fingertips until mixture looks like bread crumbs.
2. Add water, a little at a time, to make a firm (but not stiff) dough.
3. Use your hands to work the dough in bowl for about 5 or 10 minutes. Cover bowl with a clean, damp cloth and let stand for at least 1 hour.
4. Divide dough into pieces about the size of walnuts. Roll each piece into a smooth ball.
5. Sprinkle remaining flour onto a flat surface. Use a rolling pin to roll each ball into a pancake, about 1/8-inch thick.
6. Ask an adult to heat a heavy skillet over medium heat. When hot, place one chapati in the center. After about 1 minute, turn the chapati over with a spatula.
7. Cook the other side for 1 minute.
8. Cook chapatis, one at a time. Wrap them in a towel to keep warm.
9. Brush cooked chapatis with butter and serve warm.

Getting
Dressed

To beat the heat, Indians put on light-weight and loose clothing that won't stick to the body.

Traditionally, men and boys wear a *kurta*, a white cotton shirt without a collar over light cotton pants called

Dhobis

Indians who can afford to, take their dirty clothes to a laundromat, called a dhobi. Dhobi workers separate clothes by color and clothing type. They also carefully mark each piece in a coding system that only dhobi workers know. They bundle the shirts or pants together, soak them in soapy water, and then beat them long and hard with sticks. The dhobi workers dry the clothing on lines, and then they carry them to a big ironing shed. They eventually deliver the clean clothing to its owner—using the secret code for identification.

(Left) **On a visit to the Taj Mahal, these men sport traditional Indian clothing, including dhotis.**

churdiar. Many men also wrap a light cloth known as a *dhoti* around the waist and between the legs.

Indian women and girls wrap themselves in a narrow piece of cloth, about 16 feet long, called a *sari.* They hang saris around their bodies in different ways, depending on the occasion and where they live. Women also wear different colored saris to reflect moods. For example, when an Indian woman's husband dies, she is expected to wear a white sari. Many women wear their sari over a long skirt or slip, with a matching blouse to cover their shoulders.

Try This with a Bedsheet!

To wear a sari, a woman first tucks one of the ends into the top of her skirt. Then she wraps it around her body one or two times and throws the other end around her left shoulder.

Sometimes she arranges a sari over her head, too. The end of the sari hangs behind her back or around her shoulders.

Going to **School**

Kids in India start school when they are six years old. Boys and girls usually don't share the same classroom, and many girls, especially those from small villages, don't go to school at all. They stay home to help their mothers with housework.

School is hard work. The schoolday lasts from eight o'clock to noon. Lessons focus on math, Indian history, and geography. Most students also study their local dialect, Hindi, and English. Teachers give a lot of homework, and parents encourage their children to get good grades.

Counting in India

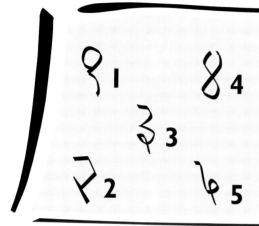

Here's how to count to five in India. The index finger pressed against the thumb means one, the middle finger pressed against the thumb means two, the ring finger means three, and the pinky means four. All the fingers pressed against the thumb means five, and the two hands held in the same way means ten.

After six years, students must score at least 70 out of 100 on a final exam to pass from grade school to secondary school. More than half of all students leave school after grade school to go to work on the family farm. Others leave school but continue to take private lessons from teachers.

(Above left) **In a typical Indian classroom, kids may sit on the floor or at desks. Sometimes classes are even held outside!** (Right) **Ten-year-old Sakina is from Takukibowli, a village not far from Varanasi. She is learning to write in Hindi, and she uses her black wooden slate to practice.**

Nights with
Lights

(Right) **Gotcha! During Holi, street vendors sell colored powders and colored waters that people use to shower their friends. This woman enjoys the celebration.**
(Below) **Sparklers brighten the night during Diwali, the festival of lights.**

You've probably heard of Mother's Day and Father's Day, but what about kid's day? Why don't they get a special day? In India they do! Once a year, the people of India celebrate Children's Day. On this day, parents hold small parties for their kids or plan other fun things to do, like taking them to the zoo or to a movie.

Have you ever had a water fight? That's kind of how Indians observe Holi, a Hindu festival that honors the passing of winter. People throw colored water or red powder at one another. After dark they light small oil lamps to mark the death of Holika, the goddess of winter. For three nights in a row, oil lamps brighten cities and villages.

Diwali, the Hindu festival of lights, takes place in October or November, during the darkest time of the year. Diwali lasts for five days. Families clean their homes, light oil lamps, exchange candies, and set off fireworks. The festival celebrates the favorite Hindu story, *Ramayana*, in which the Hindu god Rama returns home after spending 12 years in the jungle.

Women celebrate Diwali by floating candles out on a lake.

Crazy about **Cricket**

These kids have found the perfect spot for a game of cricket.

Ever since the British brought the game of cricket to India in the 1800s, Indians have been crazy about it. How is cricket played? Here's cricket in a nutshell.

Two teams of 11 players each participate in a cricket match. One team bats, while the other team fields. The batting team puts forward two batsmen at a time. The fielding team has nine fielders, a bowler (pitcher), and a wicket-keeper (catcher). At either end of the pitch (bowling area) is a wicket (base).

The bowler stands behind one

wicket. One of the batsmen is positioned in front of the other. A wicketkeeper stands behind the batsman and the wicket. The second batsman waits next to the bowler, ready to run if the first batsman should happen to hit the ball. The bowler runs up the pitch to the nearest wicket and throws the ball toward the batsman, who tries to hit it with his bat.

If the batsman hits the ball and a fielder catches it, then the batsman is out. If a fielder doesn't catch the ball, the two batsmen start to run back and forth between the wickets as fast as they can. When they reach opposite wickets and touch the ground with their bats, their team scores a run. After 10 outs, the other team comes to bat. Cricket matches can go on for as long as five days!

Professional cricket players wear white uniforms with special pads for protection.

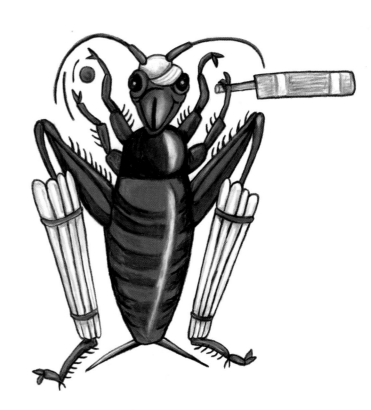

The Raj Mandir movie theater in Jaipur, India, is hopping on the weekends.

Lights! Camera! **Action!**

On a Saturday afternoon with nothing to do, most people in India would go to the movies. And they have plenty of shows to choose from. India produces more movies than any other country in the world—sometimes as many as 800 films in one year! In fact, old Bombay (modern Mumbai), where most of the movies are made, is sometimes called "Bollywood."

Indian movies are favorites outside of India, too. Movie theaters all over southern Asia and in much of Africa feature Indian movies.

What makes Indian movies so popular? People call films made in Bollywood "masala movies." Masala is a blend of Indian spices used in cooking. So Indian movies are a mixture of a little bit of everything. All movies have action, romance,

Billboards advertising the latest Hindi movies cover the side of a building in Mumbai, India.

and comedy. Each film follows a certain formula. Like Hollywood movies, good guys battle bad guys, and the good guys always win in the end. Family conflicts develop and are eventually worked out. But one thing sets many Indian films apart from the rest. Instead of speaking, Indian actors sing and dance the action of the film.

Indian Movie Stars

Movie stars in India are national heroes. Jayalalitha Jayaram—one of the country's most famous actresses—is so popular that people in Tamil Nadu elected her to serve in the local government. She's also wealthy—she owns 10,500 saris. (If Ms. Jayaram wore a different sari every day, it would take her 30 years to wear them all!)

Indian Music

Indian music might sound unfamiliar to most North Americans. Two stringed instruments, the *sitar* and the *tanpoura*, make Indian music unique. Both instruments look kind of like stretched-out guitars. A drummer determines how fast or slow the musicians should play by beating on two small drums called tabla.

The sitar player usually starts an Indian song. The sitar sounds a bit like a long high-pitched cry. Then the two other musicians join in. The tanpoura player strums a single note, over and over. The tabla

A musician plays a stringed instrument on a street in Pushkar, Rajasthan.

Drummers wear their instruments strapped over the shoulder, so they can walk and play at the same time.

player beats out a rhythm called a *tala*. The sitar player plucks his scale (string of notes), or **raga,** in time to the tala. Musicians play different ragas depending on the time of day or the season.

Do you like to dance? In India dance is considered a work of art. The ways in which the dancers move their hands, neck, and eyes all convey meaning. These women dance in saris at the Desert Festival in Rajasthan.

Glossary

caste: A social group that holds a traditional place and occupation in Hindu or Jain culture.

curry: A mixture of different spices used to flavor meat or vegetables.

desert: A dry, sandy region that receives low amounts of rainfall.

dialect: A regional variety of language with different pronunciations from other regional varieties.

ethnic group: A large community of people that shares a number of social features in common such as language, religion, or customs.

ghats: Steps leading down to the edge of a river or lake used for ritual bathing.

mehndi: The art of making designs in henna paste on the hands, feet, or other parts of the body.

Elephants were once the prized possessions of wealthy princes. This decorated elephant stands guard at the Royal Palace in Jaipur.

monsoon: A period of heavy rain brought by seasonal winds.

plain: A broad, flat area of land that has few trees or other outstanding natural features.

plateau: A large area of high, level land.

raga: A series of notes used to improvise melodies in Indian music.

shrine: A sacred place that may contain religious images.

subcontinent: A large area of land smaller than a continent.

Wearable Art

One kind of Indian art goes right on your body. It's called **mehndi,** the art of body painting.

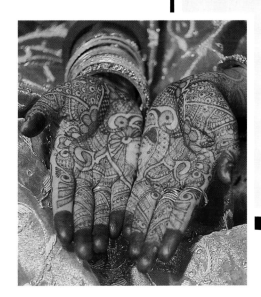

Mehndi artists use henna paste—made from the leaves of a tropical shrub—to create designs on the skin. Henna stains the skin, so when the paste is washed off, the pattern stays behind. The designs are often swirling patterns of red, pink, or orange. Mehndi designs look like fancy tattoos. But they don't hurt a bit!

People get mehndi designs for special occasions, such as weddings. The designs last about two weeks. According to tradition, new brides are excused from housework until the mehndi designs on their hands or feet wear off.

Pronunciation Guide

Adivasi	AH-dee-vah-see
Bhagavad-Gita	bah-gah-vahd GEE-tah
Brahman	BRAH-mee-nh
chapati	chah-PAH-tee
charpoy	CHAH-r-paai
churdiar	chu-REE-dahr
Diwali	dee-WAH-lee
dhoti	DH-oo-tee
Ganges	GAH-n-gah or GAN-jeez
Himalayas	himh-ah-LAYH-az
Hindi	HIHN-dee
Hindu	HIHN-doo
Hinduism	HIHN-doo-iz-em
Holi	HO-lee
Jainism	JEYE-niz-em
kshatriya	kesh-at-REE-ah
Mahabharata	mah-HAH-bha-rah-tah
masala	mah-SAH-laah
mehndi	MEH-an-dee
namaste	nah-mah-STAY
Nepal	NE-paale
Punjabi	pun-jah-BHEE
Ramayana	RAH-mah-ya-naah
Sikhism	SEE-kh-iz-em
sitar	si-TAH-r
Sri Lanka	SREE lahng-kuh
swagatam Bharat-Varsh	SWAH-ga-tahm BAH-rah-tah var-SHAH
tabla	tab-LAAH
Taj Mahal	TAAJ mah-hawl
tala	TAH-lah
Tamil Nadu	TAH-mil nah-DOO
tanpoura	than-POO-rah

Further Reading

Ardley, Bridget and Neil. *India*. People and Places series. Englewood Cliffs, NJ: Silver Burdett Press, 1989.

Axworthy, Anni. *Anni's India Diary*. New York: Whispering Coyote Press Inc., 1992.

Chenevière, Alain. *Ramachandra in India*. Minneapolis: Lerner Publications Company, 1996.

Cumming, David. *India*. Our Country series. New York: The Bookwright Press, 1991.

Ganeri, Anita. *Exploration Into India*. New York: New Discovery Books, 1994.

Ganeri, Anita and Rachel Wright. *India: Country Topics for Craft Projects*. New York: Franklin Watts, 1994.

Galbraith, Catherine Atwater and Rama Mehta. *India, Now and through Time*. Boston: Houghton Mifflin Company, 1980.

India in Pictures. Minneapolis: Lerner Publications Company, 1989.

Madavan, Vijay. *Cooking the Indian Way*. Minneapolis: Lerner Publications Company, 1985.

Severance, John B. *Gandhi: Great Soul*. New York: Clarion Books, 1997.

Tigwell, Tony. *A Family in India*. Minneapolis: Lerner Publications Company, 1985.

Metric Conversion Chart

WHEN YOU KNOW:	MULTIPLY BY:	TO FIND:
teaspoon	5.0	milliliters
Tablespoon	15.0	milliliters
cup	0.24	liters
inches	2.54	centimeters
feet	0.3048	meters
miles	1.609	kilometers
square miles	2.59	square kilometers
degrees Fahrenheit	5/9 (after subtracting 32)	degrees Celsius

Index

Adivasi, 10, 11
Aryans, 10, 13

Bay of Bengal, 5, 8
Bengalis, 13
Buddhism, 18, 21

caste system, 20–21
chapati, 30, 31
cities, 16, 24–25, 26–27
clothing, 32–33
cows, 11
cricket, 38–39

Deccan Plateau, 7
Desert of Thar, 7
dhobis, 32
Diwali, 36–37
Dravidians, 10, 13

ethnic groups, 13

families, 24, 28–29
farmers, 9, 22
food, 30–31

Ganesh, 16–17
Ganges, 6, 8, 9, 18

Himalayas, 6, 8
Hindi, 5, 14–15

Hinduism, 8, 18–19, 20
Holi, 37
holidays, 36–37
homeless people, 24, 25
houses, 22–23

Indo–Gangetic Plain, 6–7
Indus, 7, 8–9

Jainism, 19, 20

languages, 5, 10, 13, 14–15,
    29, 34

map of India, 4
marriages, 28–29
mehndi, 45
monsoons, 9
mountains, 6–7
movies, 40–41
music, 42–43

people, 10–11, 12–13, 24–25
population, 24–25

religions, 8, 12, 13, 18–19
rivers, 6–7, 8–9

saris, 33
schools, 34–35
shoes, 23

Sikhs, 13
sports, 38–39
squatters, 24, 25

Taj Mahal, 27
Tamils, 13
towns, 22–23, 26–27
travel methods, 16–17

untouchables, 20, 21

varnas, 21